Meditation for Everyone

Your Secular Guide to Spiritual Growth

Lou McCall

PixelCircus

MEDITATION FOR EVERYONE: YOUR SECULAR GUIDE TO
SPIRITUAL GROWTH

This book is dedicated to my loving partner, Peter. Without his big heart, generous spirit, and unfailing support this book could not have been written.

Contents

Foreword

I wish I had this book when I first read about meditation as a teenager and yearned to know how. It was too soon: the Beatles hadn't begun their music career and introducing Maharishi Mahesh Yogi to the world was still years off.

It wasn't until 1974 that I learned how to meditate. I dove in, and it was a homecoming. It took years and many books to answer my questions about this mysterious, peaceful, creativity-enhancing way of life. And still, when I read meditation teacher, Lou McCall's in-depth guide, *Meditation for Everyone,* there was new information for me. For you, it's all here in one book.

There is so much more to meditation than calming the mind and going within. These pages are a treasure trove, not just clear instructions but also teachings on meditation's many aspects and how daily practice can radically change your life.

Meditation is how we get to know our minds and it helps us more effectively respond to life's challenges. By discovering the nature of reality through daily meditation, we can achieve the peace and personal growth that boosts us from merely existing to living fully, even experiencing joy for no reason!

In fascinating and compelling ways, McCall explains the who, what, when, where, why, and how: what meditation is (and isn't), when is the most effective time, where to meditate, why meditate at all, and most importantly, how to do it.

If you have never meditated, this fun-to-read book is for you. Who benefits from meditation? Everyone! From children to teenagers to middle-aged folks to those at the end of their lives. What better way to leave this world than to still our mind and witness with clarity our last moments?

If you have not meditated for a while, this book will inspire you to renew your practice; it will remind you of its benefits and applying its teachings will help you get started again. I invite you to soak up Lou's wisdom and reap the endless rewards meditation has to offer.

Ellen Wood
Questa, New Mexico

Introduction

> "If every 8-year-old in the world is taught meditation, it will eliminate violence from the world within one generation."
>
> —*His Holiness, the 14th Dalai Lama*

I began writing this book as a resource for my meditation students, a basic tool that was not affiliated with any group, organization, or philosophy. I wanted a simple hand-out, a take-home guide to support their personal meditation practice. It began as a page or two of basic guidelines to get them started and to help them continue meditating.

My conviction, born from my own experience and that of my teachers and students, is that the practice of meditation is a panacea, not only for personal ills, but for global ones as well. I spent many years engaged in political, social, and environmental activism. I felt it was my personal responsibility to do my part to make the world a better place. When one cares about our magnificent planet and its interdependent inhabitants, doing something beneficial to protect and nurture them can give one a sense of purpose and hope. I found that not taking any action at all led to feelings of helplessness and despair.

I later learned, both from experience and through my studies of spiritual psychology, that these negative emotions such as helplessness were key causal factors for depression, as well as for alienation and isolation. I believe we all have a significant role to play; the world is not complete without us. If you watch the news, you know that every day it is becoming more critical that we, that is, everyone, on this small planet, learn the lessons of how to live together and share our finite resources. To do this, from a personal to a global level, we must find peace within. Only through this inner process can we become clear as to our purpose in making the world a better place.

When I began putting this book together in 2013, I realized that it marked my 40th anniversary as a meditator. With this edition, I celebrate half a century of meditation practice, wow!

When I first read Hermann Hesse's book, *Siddhartha,* in high school, I woke up to a whole world of possibilities that were available to me; the book was an eye-opener. Or as we said in the 1970s "It blew my mind." I was stunned by it and still remember the day I finished reading it. I felt the need to take a walk and sit quietly beneath a tree to contemplate the book's profound message and its impact on me; it changed my world view.

In my first year of college, I saw a flyer announcing a class on Transcendental Meditation, known as TM. I showed up, learned the technique, and have been meditating ever since. Taking this weekend workshop was a personal pivot point. It introduced me as a teenager to a level of awareness that I didn't know existed. Exploring consciousness became a lifetime passion.

Meditation is not only a historic and traditional part of countless cultures, religions and philosophies, it has also became a megalithic industry. While meditation is inherently valuable in countless ways, it has found commercial success in the marketplace. This is a good thing, reaching many more people and becoming more accepted and accessible —that is, as long as the teachings are not adulterated by greed and corruption. In the late 20th century traditional teachings became a key element of a counterculture that became available to me and seekers like me. It speaks well of our times that meditation is no longer a fringe movement, but broadly accepted in mainstream thought and culture.

Since my first experience with TM, I have studied meditation with many teachers and learned from different traditions. The practice of meditation has been a blessing to me and has brought immeasurable peace, well-being and improved health. I believe that I am a more conscious individual, and more sensitive and compassionate because of my meditation practice. I also believe that my meditation has made a difference to those around me; I am a better friend and listener. I am happier, too.

My study of meditation has been a lifetime journey that introduced me to different people, cultures, and ways of thought. Throughout my many-faceted life, through different locales and career changes, physical challenges and all kinds of work, hobbies, and interests, I have meditated. Once I found this inner resource, I was never the same. I was lucky because I started exploring this territory at a young age. When I moved away from home to a bigger city, I landed in a community where meditation was an integral and accepted part of daily life; it was not exotic and whacky. Initially I was shy and too embarrassed to talk about my newfound passion. Whenever I realized that I was in the presence of a fellow meditator, I felt a sense of connection and belonging, of having found my tribe. Knowing I was not alone or weird helped me overcome long standing feelings of isolation.

Through continued study and dedication to the practice I felt stronger, more stable, and not so alone. As a child, I was neither happy nor healthy; I grew up in a family plagued with substance abuse, depression and undiagnosed mental illness, issues that I inherited and took on as my own. It was only later, through a commitment to personal growth, that I was able to identify and understand the ramifications of my family drama in my own life. There is power in each of us and feeling empowered is one of the outcomes from a sustained meditation practice.

As my own meditation practice deepened, my commitment to it grew. I came to understand that meditating and teaching meditation was the most important thing I could do to bring harmony to our troubled world. That's a big claim, I know. I truly believe that finding that peaceful space inside us is the only way to create peace on the planet. I am such a believer in the power of meditation that I can say without a doubt that everyone could benefit from the practice, and the planet will benefit, too. What troubles in the world do not arise from fear, ignorance, greed and unhappiness?

One of my Buddhist teachers, on reading an early manuscript of this book, expressed concern that my conviction may set up such high expectations that readers could easily get disappointed and disillusioned with meditation, that someone just learning may get the impression that meditation is supposed to be easy, or that it doesn't work or perhaps is over-rated. That is a valid point. Nowhere in this book is it written that meditation is easy. It is simple, though.

Meditation is a process that must be practiced with diligence and regularity. It takes months, years, decades and maybe lifetimes to explore all the dimensions that meditation offers. One must start some place. It is my hope that this book be a launching point for those who read it; I hope they dedicate themselves to the practice and witness for themselves the fruits of their efforts.

As a way of celebrating now five decades of meditation practice, I am happy that I can share this book with you. I hope it inspires you, not only to practice meditating, but to make it an essential part of your life. Let's help make meditation a widespread practice that is integrated into the fabric of the culture we live in.

May all beings benefit.

Chapter 1

Who?

"We are human beings, not human doings."

—Author Unknown

As the title *Meditation for Everyone* suggests, it is my belief that there is absolutely no one who cannot benefit from the practice of meditation. Throughout the thousands of years that Earthlings have been engaged in the practice of one form of meditation or another, it has been the common ground of all wisdom traditions. We explore in depth the definition of what meditation is in the "What" section, coming up next. For now, let's just say that meditation is a contemplative practice to still and quiet the mind.

I believe that meditation is a basic ability that is hard wired into our physiology; it can create demonstrable benefits for both body and mind. The practice both trains the chaotic mind and calms it. Even after achieving enlightenment, the great masters still spend their time in meditation. People intuitively find themselves seeking quiet and solitude to balance their body, mind, and spirit. Meditation is truly for everyone, especially now, in these fast-paced, chaotic, and troubled times. For those who feel the call, have the interest, curiosity and will, embarking on the practice of meditation may be the most natural route toward a more harmonious future.

Some people find it extremely difficult to sit quietly in stillness to calm their minds, mainly because it is unfamiliar and therefore perhaps uncomfortable. Yet with sustained effort and a commitment to practice, they can meditate with a degree of effectiveness and satisfaction. Being calm is a habit that can be cultivated, both on and off the meditation seat.

Meditation is a suitable activity for all people, regardless of age, gender, culture, or lifestyle. It is a universal truth that we can all understand — you may find that you have the ability to train your mind and find peace. Depressed or anxious persons especially may find relief through meditation. It might be the perfect thing to do if you are ill or recovering from an accident or trauma.

A few years after I started meditating, I was in a life-changing auto accident; I broke my neck, both my hips and sustained severe head injuries. It is not clear if I was in a coma for ten days or if I was heavily drugged to prevent me from moving. That I survived earned me the nickname with the hospital staff "The Good Karma Kid." I vowed to live up to that title.

I was told that I would be in the hospital for a minimum of three months; I was admitted the day before Thanksgiving and left the day after Christmas, so it was only one month, which felt miraculous. I was told it would take years to recover and yes, that may be partially true; being young and resilient at age 25, I managed to get back on my feet much faster than predicted.

I was also told that I would never have the full use of my partially paralyzed arms, and with the help of many health care professionals, I gave meaning to the term, fake it till you make it. My gratitude for anyone in health care professions is immense, especially for nurses and all those who helped me on my path to healing. I fully realized that with their support, the healing process was all mine, it was my responsibility, and I took it seriously. With little else to do in the early days of recovery, I had the only tool I needed — meditation.

I had a dear friend who came to visit me almost every day in the hospital. When I started reading, he brought me all manner of inspirational books. Until that point my understanding of meditation was purely experiential and I didn't know that I could read about meditation to further my understanding. Books by Stephen Levine and Joseph

Goldstein I remember as being truly uplifting. I also owe a great debt of gratitude to Shakti Gawain, whose work with creative visualization helped me envision a future beyond my injuries. Thus began the next leg of my journey, please pardon the pun!

Transcendental Meditation teaches that one may meditate more than twice a day if sick or injured and I found it to be a priceless tool in my recovery. The health effects of a relaxed body and mind cannot be overstated. Healing is the natural result of conscious rest. I recommend meditation to anyone who is faced with any challenging condition, of body, mind or emotion.

Has anyone NOT experienced a condition that needed healing? As we unconsciously lead our lives, sometimes we are so caught up in external concerns that we are unaware of stressful circumstances challenging or preventing our well-being. Meditation helps us tune in to what is happening in a mindful way, to hear the whispers of wisdom warning us of danger or directing us to the path that is right for us. If we are unconscious of that inner compass and ignore guidance or warning, life has a way of stopping us in our tracks. That is what happened to me when I had the accident. I had no choice but to consciously stop and redirect my life.

Meditation is available to everyone who wants to get to know themselves and improve their lives in any way. It is increasingly difficult to ignore the role that stress plays in creating negative outcomes – to our health, relationships, in every sphere of experience. The health of body, mind and spirit as well as healthy interactions and societies is reliant on a certain level of happiness that is only possible with lowered levels of stress and anxiety. Peace and contentment are a worthy goal and to some may seem out of reach in our overstimulated society, but they are there, waiting for us to discover them hidden under the layers.

Who hasn't been consumed with worry, fear, or anxiety? Unfortunately, concern for the future is a fact of life. Most of us have kept ourselves up at night because we cannot turn off thoughts and concerns about the future. What we put our attention on tends to help usher it into our lives. Worry is prayer for what we DON'T want! And we also stress about the past, with regrets about what we did or didn't do with obsessive thoughts about what we wished we had done instead. Being stuck in the past is a real thing for a lot of people. The more we focus on the past, the less available we are to be fully present and aware, right here and right now.

Buddhists say that there are only two truly profound moments in life: birth and death. Any woman who has given birth knows how profound that moment can be. They find that focusing the mind on the breath and on the moment, makes a big difference in the birthing process. For those facing the end of their life, meditation might be one of the bravest and kindest things they can do, not only for themselves but for their loved ones and those around them.

For those who are not accustomed to being alone or have a fear of solitude, meditation can be an opportunity for overcoming that obstacle to self-realization.

Meditation for Addiction

Meditation can be the very key to recovery for those struggling to break a drug, alcohol, or tobacco habit. In fact, meditation can help with any habitual tendency. All successful recovery programs have an essential spiritual or self-awareness component. Most of our habits are mindless, automatic reactions and much easier to overcome with mindful awareness. Addiction has been the topic of countless scientific studies which conclude that it is a serious health problem with very strong physical components. It is also said that addiction is a spiritual disease. When we feel that we absolutely must have something, and we have no control over our urges, it may indicate some unfulfilled need that cannot be satisfied with a temporary or external fix.

Next time you feel an urge to indulge in your poison, try sitting down to meditate. You may get much the same results without the uncomfortable side effects. Watch the process of your craving, observe it in your mind and your body with curiosity. Watch it as an objective non-participant. Try not to run blindly toward your addiction without contemplating it internally. You may at least gain a new understanding and relationship with yourself and the object of your craving.

Be especially aware of the breath. Anytime you get anxious and start to react, take a few deep breaths to get centered. And focus on your exhalation, try to lengthen it. The ancient teachings say that this calms you down. This is a secret tool that is available to everyone. One of the benefits of meditation is that you may learn to be more aware of your breathing and more in tune with your physical body. With practice you may find yourself noticing the quality of your breath during your daily activities, not just on the meditation seat.

And meditation is free, unlike addictive substances! Consider taking the money you save by not hurting your-self with harmful substances and use it for something nurturing, such as a massage, a class, a trip to the beach or lunch with a friend. Our materialistic culture tells us to feel and believe that we always need something more, that we are somehow lacking. Maybe we feel unworthy, or we want material things that we cannot afford, or feel that we must have a drink or a cigarette. Without true self-aware-ness, we may spend our entire lives looking outside ourselves to fill that void. Once we discover that a relation-ship with ourselves, our own mind or our Higher Power is what we truly lack, the effects can bring true jubilation.

For those who do not understand the term "Higher

Power" or for those who take issue with the semantics, please know that this is a useful term that describes feeling good and avoids any religious connotations. Higher Power could mean our love of life, or our best self, or our joy of being here now or our feelings of connection. Just as we have low days, we may also have days that seem higher – higher energy, better moods, or a greater sense of joy and well-being.

Make the effort to form good habits that make you feel better. Make a habit of meditating every day or twice a day. Start right now, today with the simple instructions in this book. Seek out a qualified teacher to guide you further. Find whatever support you need to keep meditating. Attend a meditation group, read books, or watch videos to further your understanding. Go on a retreat if you can. Meditation is a valuable pursuit and worth the investment of your time and effort.

For those who are extremely active, meditation brings balance to one's life. Standing meditation is taught in most martial arts training. Often during retreats sitting meditation alternates with walking meditation. Obstacles to sitting meditation may be overcome with practice. As the great masters have told us, the harder it is for you to sit and meditate, the more essential the practice may be for you.

Since this book is called *Meditation for Everyone,* I want to leave no one out. If you are incarcerated or institutionalized in any way, you have an excellent opportunity to practice. Think of the similarities between prisons and monasteries. If you have your own room or cell, you are especially well situated to begin your practice. Having a structured schedule and environment can work to your advantage, and if there is a chaplain or counselor to guide you, ask them about meditation. There are organizations that have for decades been teaching meditation in prisons for free with transformational results.

In public schools, detention has more and more been replaced by meditation, it is demonstrating positive outcomes to solve behavioral and disciplinary problems. Meditation may be the key to helping young people stay in school and avoid being at risk of leading a troubled or even dangerous life. Find what is available in your institution or invite organizations to come to work with you. In this way, you might turn time into a beneficial experience. My sincere wish is that this book finds its way into every kind of environment and may make a positive difference in someone's life.

Chapter Summary: Who?

Meditation is helpful if you:

1. Want more happiness, harmony, feelings of connection or positivity in your life.
2. Are tired, sick, have health problems or are recovering from injury or trauma.
3. Experience stress or anxiety.
4. Want to calm your mind.
5. Are often angry, upset or overwhelmed.
6. Are struggling to break an addiction or other habits.
7. Want to improve your memory and brain function.
8. Want to sleep better.
9. Want to deepen your understanding of yourself and life.
10. Are facing the end of your life or that of someone you know.
11. Are incarcerated or institutionalized.

Chapter 2

What?

med-i-tate *verb:* **To spend time in quiet thought, to think deeply, or to focus one's mind, as a method of relaxation or for spiritual purposes.**

Such is the dictionary's definition—apparently written by scholars who do not meditate. In the hope that the authors of our dictionaries will someday start meditating, they may come to redefine meditation. Most authorities on meditation today, as well as the ancient traditions from which these teachings spring, would challenge the idea that meditation is about thinking or contemplation in the conventional sense. One of my favorite slogans is, "Meditation: It's not what you think!" Tibetan Buddhist teacher, Chögyam Trungpa Rinpoche described meditation as contented cows in a lush meadow.

Meditation is a natural practice that confers a variety of

benefits. For some, it may be widely considered a religious practice, and in some parts of the world it is an important component of religion. Christians may call it *centering prayer* or *contemplative prayer*. If prayer is reaching out to God, then meditation is God reaching out to us. You could say that prayer is talking to God and meditation is listening to what God has to say.

We will take a deep dive into how to meditate in the chapter entitled *How?* For those who want to get started right away, here is the long story short about how to begin to meditate.

• Find a quiet place where you can sit quietly without interruption or distraction. Close the door, turn off your phone and other devices.

• Get comfortable and make sure you can sit without moving for a few minutes. Whether in a chair or on the floor, sit up tall, shoulders back, chin slightly tucked in and down. Your feet are grounded on the floor if you are in a chair, if seated on a cushion, elevate your hips with a pillow or cushion.

• Allow the tip of your tongue to rest lightly on the roof of your mouth, behind your upper front teeth. Close your eyes, or find a soft, lowered gaze and bring your awareness inward. Settle in and rest comfortably.

• The most convenient and universal object of focus is your breath. It is always there. Inhale and as you exhale, see if you can release any tension, worry or even thoughts. Silently observe your breath going in and out. See if you can fix your attention only on the breath. Thoughts and distractions will intrude. Gently, bring your attention back to the breath. It is very simple, but not necessarily easy. Keep practicing and don't be hard on yourself if your attention wanders.

• Feel the sensations of the breath in your nostrils, follow it into your lungs or watch your belly expand and contract in synchrony with your breath.

• I have read that it takes about seven minutes of stillness for our nervous system to shift gears; if possible, sit it out for at least that long and see if you feel the shift. Meditation should be pleasant, so sit as long as you are comfortable; even if you start with one or two minutes of stillness, that is a start. Like any muscle, you can strengthen your practice with repetition. No matter how long you meditate, make it a regular daily habit.

• Meditating for 15 -20 minutes is ideal, you could set a timer and if that is too long, no worries, don't put yourself down. You might affirm to yourself, "I can't meditate for 15 minutes - YET!" As time goes by you may find yourself wanting to extend your practice even longer. Time will go by anyway, so you may as well be meditating!

• Don't begin the practice with any great expectations. The key is to "just be," release and let go into the here and now. And be consistent and patient. The key to mindfulness is to simply pay attention and be present with exactly what is happening right now.

• There are many, many approaches to meditation, depending on the tradition or who you talk to. This is a simple way to get started, enjoy!

So, that is the "Let's get started right now version" of how to meditate. Read on to fill in the blanks and answer any questions that may come up. If you haven't done sitting meditation before, you are in the right place. Hopefully, this book inspires you to make it an important part of your life.

While meditation is an essential element of Buddhism, Hinduism, Taoism, and probably most other "isms" or religious practices, and it is true that meditation can enrich any belief system, it also enhances the practice of life itself, apart from any religion or philosophy. More and more people in the West are discovering the secular practice of meditation to become more mindful in every aspect of their lives. There are mainstream magazines on grocery newsstands about mindfulness, there are accreditation programs for teaching it to kids, and it is wonderful to see celebrities talking about meditation in interviews. It is a nonreligious practice that is now widely recognized as a simple way to alleviate stress, improve health, and achieve new levels of happiness and clarity.

The word *mindfulness* or the words *insight meditation* are heard more and more, as people consciously take steps to learn how to be in the present moment. Being in the here and now, paying attention to what is happening within us and around us, is being recognized as the practice to eliminate stress and anxiety and to become healthier and happier. I have heard mindfulness defined as "paying attention, on purpose with calmness and curiosity."

We can train our mind to be fully present, right here and right now, just by practicing, either on or off the meditation seat. We can arrive into the here and now through our breath, anchoring our awareness in our bodies. Are you worried about the future? Take a moment to come into the present moment, take a breath and be in the moment.

The same is true for dwelling on the past. If going over past events disturbs your mind, let it go and come into the beauty of the present moment. Forgive those past experiences. If you notice yourself judging, either yourself or another, train your mind to automatically forgive, rather than automatically judging. The Course in Miracles says, "Forgiveness is the key to happiness."

By paying attention to the present moment, to be fully engaged in it, we come to understand our true nature, unobstructed by the baggage that we have collected along our way. There is the relative reality of ourselves and our lives and the ultimate reality that we strive to know and understand, both of which may become clear to us through the objective observation of the mind during meditation. Focusing on the here and now clarifies the actual nature of our mind and experience, the proximate and the immediate; we free ourselves from the unreliable memories of the past and predictions and projections of the future. In other words, the stories that we make up about what happened to us before or what will happen next no longer plague us and distort our awareness right now.

Approaching life as an observer may greatly simplify your emotional well-being. Taking the situations and events of your life personally is a common cause for conflict, both internally and with others. Self-observation is not the same as clinging to your ego and being self-absorbed. It is the act of watching everything that goes on around you and within you. Watch, as if it is happening to someone else or on a movie screen. You don't have to form an opinion or judge it good or bad, or elaborate some story or drama about it. See if you can observe what is going on around you with passive detachment without getting emotionally engaged.

A good example is watching the news and being triggered by a person or situation that always seems to rile you up. If it's any consolation, a difficult person may rejoice that they are commanding your attention ant that they have gotten to you. We do not have to give them that satisfaction, real or imagined! By observing what triggers us, being aware of our reaction and letting go of our clinging to it, we may find ourselves sighing with relief. We might develop a Teflon personality, nothing sticks!

Watch your fears, cravings, and passions, just notice them for what they are, a fleeting story in your mind. You can't touch them, and they have no substance. They have no power over you, just let them go. You can also let go of your need to control events or situations. This is probably different from our usual thinking. Let go of clutching your emotional story. With improved faculties of observation, you can better discern the facts and the true nature of what is going on in your life. In so doing, the stories don't arise or don't have as much power over you. With continued practice, observation may become part of your meditation that easily transfers into your everyday life.

For indeed, what is more real than right now? It is surprising how bringing our consciousness to the present moment brings realization of what is truly going on with us and around us, thereby freeing us from the burdens of our self-composed narratives about before or after. Meditation is essentially about being aware, or mindful, of our current experience. It is a wonderful way to accept and enjoy being with life just as it is.

Think of meditation as a beneficial habit to improve life on every level. Doctors and therapists recommend it for stress-related conditions, which constitute the majority of our illnesses, at least in the developed world. It is being promoted as an excellent way to relieve stress.

Meditation is increasingly the subject of scientific research, from psychology to neurology to general medicine. What I find fascinating and affirming are the brain studies being done on Buddhist monks as they meditate with fMRIs, EKGs, and other scanning technologies. The results are clear — regular practice relieves stress, improves concentration, quiets the mind, relaxes the body, and promotes good health and vitality. It can both increase energy and improve our sleep. More and more research has discovered that meditation can actually change the structure of our brains and repair DNA. These studies have even linked meditation to longevity. As science delves deeper into the mind it is uncovering what the wise masters have known for millennia. The scientific community is now confirming what the ancients have always known!

These studies in brain science offer insight into brain waves and how they relate to mental states. Practicing meditation can help regulate brain waves, accessing different states of consciousness. Most of us in daily alert waking consciousness have brain waves oscillating in the beta state, in sync with the busy world around us. Beta waves are often linked to stress and anxiety. A slower wave is Alpha, associated with calm relaxation; in meditation our brain waves may eventually slow into Theta waves. The Theta state is what we associate with meditation, creativity, and dreaming. The slowest brain waves are Delta, associated with deep sleep and are essential to healing the body.

Gamma brain waves have the highest frequency of brain waves and are associated with high levels of thought and focus. In the Gamma state you might say that your brain is firing on all cylinders, signaling peak concentration. High levels of gamma waves may tend to increase happiness and receptivity. Long time meditators, such as Buddhist monks have been studied and demonstrate a state known as Gamma synchrony. In this super-conscious state, there is a coordination or syncopation of neural networks, fancy science talk for "having it all together."

Most meditators report calm states of awareness, such as in the Theta state. Finding oneself in the super conscious Gamma state may not be immediately accessible, at least not for most of us. Knowing about brain waves may be helpful for understanding the state of our minds during meditation, as well as in waking states and even sleep.

Meditation is being championed in the workplace to increase productivity. Corporations such as Forbes have found that employee satisfaction, health and happiness is enhanced with meditation. It helps with stress management to improve mental health and cognition. Surprisingly, prejudice is reduced due to enhanced empathy and compassion. Meditation can enrich collaboration among co-workers and has been found to help boost memory and curb emotional reactions. Big business is investing in employee well-being to increase their bottom line! You could say meditation is a gateway drug; it is introduced for material benefit and opens a whole new world of consciousness and benefits. I like to think of a transformed global economy as a side effect of a more conscious workplace.

There has been some criticism from traditional scholars that meditation is being taken out of context. They say it should be a spiritual practice, not a secular one, and belongs in the spiritual traditions from which they came. No one owns the rights to meditation, or should I say, everyone owns the right to meditation? In the natural world, we see dogs and cats and probably all living beings sitting quietly. Maybe meditation is entirely natural and is a universal ability of all conscious beings. We humans have the ability to bring ourselves to this natural state, although it is not always culturally sanctioned or taught, at least not in the Western world. That is changing!

The Busy Sickness

In the old days when someone was asked how they were

doing, they would reply, "Fine." Now the standard automatic response is "Busy," which is sometimes code for too busy to stop and have a real conversation or connection. Having too much to do and rushing about has become a large part of our reality. People complain about it, and other than that, it isn't part of the bigger conversation, especially regarding the harmful effects this chaos has on our individual psyches and our culture. Hurry is not the friend of a peaceful life.

Unlike dogs and cats, we are busy thinking and doing, more so than feeling and being. We have forgotten the ability to bring ourselves into natural states of relaxation. In humankind's progress into the 21st century, I have felt like the cosmic wheels have accelerated. I didn't have any evidence, but that is what it felt like. Don't we all feel like time is going faster and it is getting harder and harder to keep up? I attributed that to globalization and the sheer volume of stimulation that comes our way every day resulting in so many of us feeling frazzled and unable to keep up.

And then I was given a book written by physicist Carlo Rovelli called *The Order of Time.* Although I cannot pretend to understand much of the book, it did make clear that yes, time is definitely going faster, and it is not just in our imaginations. It is an exciting topic now for scientific research. Some say it makes sense with an expanding universe that time itself would accelerate. I will leave it to the experts and their mathematical equations to make their case. It is comforting to know that it is not just me, time really is going faster!

What if we could stop time or slow it down by sitting in meditation? When we withdraw our senses from the external world and bring our awareness inward, time continues but it has no hold on us. We do not need to be caught up in it.

More and more, our busy culture and everyone who subscribes to the overwhelm becomes increasingly disconnected from the natural state that is the true ground of our being. The affects may show up in our lives as feelings of overwhelm, discomfort, illness, or chaos, what we call craziness. Craziness has become the norm, unfortunately, with devastating results, both individually and collectively.

Throughout history, in most wisdom traditions, being cloistered with a minimum of contact with the outside world, was the key to finding inner peace and enlightenment. This is also true for mountain yogis and others not affiliated with religions; those rogue holy men and women who escape the demands of civilization and its fascinations.

It is a good thing that retreats of all kinds are becoming more available. Meditation and yoga retreats, mental health retreats, drug rehabilitation retreats, writing retreats, and even retreats to help us break away and detox ourselves from technology. There is something to be said for taking a break from the overstimulation that for many plays too big a role in our lives. There is wisdom to the phrase, "Stop the world, I want to get off." Although as far as I know, no one has yet figured out how to stop the world, we can step back from it and to some degree stop our engagement with it.

It is true that inner peace is beneficial to world peace and vice versa. Wouldn't it be a wonderful world if people chose leaders who were peaceful and happy inside, who were motivated by having the best interests of all beings and the planet in mind? Imagine what they could bring to the world stage.

More and more, the Hurry Disease is a concern for individuals as well as medical professionals. Stress related illnesses are symptoms, and the U.S. is more afflicted than other parts of the globe. Being overwhelmed and forgetful, with feelings of frustration and hopelessness are just some of the qualities that lead to a life without peace, joy, or happiness. Thomas Merton says in his book *Conjectures of a Guilty Bystander*,

> "There is a pervasive form of contemporary violence to which the idealist most easily succumbs: activism and overwork. The rush and pressure of modern life are a form, perhaps the most common form, of its innate violence. To allow oneself to be carried away by a multi-

tude of conflicting concerns, to surrender to too many demands, to commit oneself to too many projects, to want to help everyone in everything, is to succumb to violence. The frenzy of our activism neutralizes our work for peace. It destroys our inner capacity for peace. It destroys the fruitfulness of our own work, because it kills the root of inner wisdom which makes work fruitful."

Merton is not painting activism with a negative brush; around the world concerned citizens act for truth and justice with positive outcomes. Merton is warning us against taking action in a frenzied way, that being pushed too hard in many directions and succumbing to anger can limit our effectiveness, with a violent affect on our psyches and the cultures we live in.

We wonder why there is so much violence in the world. For some reason, the media spends hundreds of billions of dollars to produce "entertainment" about guns, bombs and killing other beings, mostly people. This chaos occurs when a culture is in trouble. It is an early indicator of a failed state. The fall of the Roman Empire, in which gladiators killed people for sport and entertainment is a blatant example.

In the United States, with the average child witnessing thousands of murders on television, movies, and games, even before he or she leaves elementary school, it isn't surprising that these "games" are enacted in real life. This is one reason why there is so much violence reported on the news every day. Citing history as an example, for eons human beings have been fascinated by violence – war, murder, etc. Newsrooms say, "If it bleeds, it leads." That is unfortunate that our culture seems to be obsessed and addicted to bad news. Perhaps we would all be happier if we made it a point to expose ourselves to more good news.

Violent entertainment is loud, even harmful to the ears; the soundtracks feature gunshots, punches and kicks, shrieks, moans and groans of pain, car crashes, bombs, explosions, and destruction of every kind. Is it any wonder that the sounds in our minds are so noisy and chaotic, destructive even? Meditation quiets our minds. Turn off the world, withdraw the senses and turn within; the yogis call this, *pratyahara,* letting go of the grip that our senses have over us. The peace is there, we just need to sit with it, to patiently find it within and connect with it. Enjoy it!

Whoever you are and whatever your meditation goals, the practice starts with the ability to slow down and still the mind. The energy in the body responds to one's surroundings and one's state of mind. When one is tense or afraid, the energy contracts and stagnates; when one is quiet and still, the energy circulates freely. One may even say that experiences and circumstances respond to our state of mind. One of my favorite quotes from Lao Tzu is, "To the mind that is still, the whole universe surrenders."

Many students of meditation experience spontaneous movement of energy in their bodies. Blocks and obstructions in our nervous system or the release of tension in our muscles could be attributed to relaxing and letting go. According to Oriental medicine, some people experience an opening of one or several acupuncture meridians. The same is true of the chakras, which in the yogic tradition are the energy vortices located along the spine, associated with the endocrine glands.

How do we still our minds? By feeling peaceful. How to find peace? By taking care of yourself. Self-care is a buzz term now, thank God, everyone is talking about it and not a minute too soon! Just like in an airplane when the flight attendant demonstrates how to use the oxygen mask, the key point is to put your own mask on first, before you try to help others with their mask... You are no good to yourself or others if you don't care for yourself.

The cure for Busy Sickness, or the Hurry Sickness, or whatever you want to call it is self-care.

Many of the ailments that we experience are direct results of hurry, stress, fatigue, and depletion. It is no wonder that external demands are such that care and feeding of the human body and soul go neglected. Healing is a natural consequence of conscious rest.

Self-care can take many forms. Getting enough sleep is key. Proper nutrition, good clean food, exercise, and stress reduction are essential. Spend enough time with friends, family and pets. Allow yourself enough Me Time, set boundaries and make sure you have time and energy to build resilience, good health and happiness. For many taking a vacation is a luxury or not an option; at least spend time outdoors, in nature, and call it a mini vacation. Or what about a Stay-cation? If you can't get away, try taking time off to do a little retreat at home, catching up on sleep, projects, self-care, maybe even unplugging your devices and spending time meditating.

It is no surprise that meditation can be such a valuable self-care tool. Being good stewards of our bodies means paying attention to its needs and listening to its signals. When you chaotically run from one stimulus to another, it is difficult to listen to what your body is telling you. When you quiet your mind, you can hear your body whispering to you. It is so important to hear those whispers; please do not make your body raise its voice to you! Be a body listener.

Meditation is extremely simple, but not necessarily easy. For most people, especially in the West, the concept of doing nothing can be problematic. While we are called human beings, most of us are actually human doings! The first thing people ask others when they meet is "What do you do?" And our identities of who we are, are wrapped up in what we do.

It is important to switch from doing to simply being.

Anyone who has tried to sit quietly in meditation can testify how hard it is to turn off their habitual mental activity. As we sit, lists are made in our mind about what we should be doing, making it hard to focus on what we are doing, which we may judge as nothing. The contemplation of nothingness can be profound.

Meditation is not really "doing nothing." When we sit in stillness, with our own body, breath and mind, there is a lot going on. First, we need to be functionally able to sit in stillness for extended periods. The ancients discovered yoga to get the body in shape for sitting meditation. As we sit and bring our awareness to our body, breath, and mind in this present moment, we can let go of the grip that the workaday world has on us. As we calmly observe our breath and inquire within, what is outside of us fades into the background, we can detach and let go of its hold on us.

People who have tried to meditate and found it difficult may say, "That doesn't work for me, my meditation is running, or dancing, or working in the garden." Lots of pastimes can be meditative activities that are beneficial for our health and well-being. Listening to guided recordings to help us relax or focus our minds, getting lost in the zone while running, awash in oxygen and endorphins, or engaged in other meditative activities such as gardening or spending time in nature are important. They are all worthy endeavors that support the sitting practice and can help us stay happy and healthy. And sitting meditation complements other practices like tai chi, chi kung and yoga, as well as sports and creative endeavors like art and music.

In this book, we are talking about silent meditation, sitting in quiet stillness. To some that may seem like a narrow definition of meditation. With time and a commitment to regular practice you may find that the process can help add a meditative quality to your other activities, improving them greatly.

Chapter Summary: What?

What is meditation:

1. Sitting quietly.
2. Becoming an observer of the events of your life.
3. Watching the breath.
4. Observing the mind.
5. Detaching from the past and future.
6. Being in the here and now.
7. Letting go of resistance.
8. Letting go of expectations.
9. Focus and concentration.
10. Letting go of the exterior world and its grip on us, eliminating the cause of Hurry Sickness.

Chapter 3

When?

"Every moment is a gift, that's why it is called the present."

—Author Unknown

To the highly achieved meditation master the answer to the question, "When?" is every moment. For the rest of us, well... the answer is at least once a day, preferably twice. It is widely taught that meditation is the best way to begin our day, as a way of tuning up for the day ahead. It is best practiced first thing in the morning, on an empty stomach, before breakfast. When we first wake up our minds are generally already quiet, and the time spent meditating can go quickly. Because meditation can be a deeply restful state, sometimes even more so than sleep, it is worth getting up a little earlier to spend twenty minutes or so meditating before starting the day. Try setting your alarm for a half hour earlier and see what happens.

It is helpful to meditate when we wake up before we engage in conversation, watch the news, jump onto our computers, or get overly caffeinated. Once the outer chatter begins, the inner is sure to follow. Monasteries and retreat centers often observe "noble silence" until after the morning meditation or breakfast.

Ideally, meditation is best practiced on an empty stomach, at least for beginners. Seasoned masters probably have gone beyond those kinds of physical limitations–we may never know! Practicing before breakfast and dinner is ideal, if that works for you and your lifestyle. Meditating on a full stomach can make you drowsy, your body's energy is going toward digestion in your stomach and not to your higher brain centers.

It is also important to make sure you are well-hydrated before you begin. Drinking a glass of water helps all those neurological functions connect and improve cognitive abilities. In fact, your entire physiological system may thank you. Being hydrated is an essential aspect of being alive and can contribute to your well-being on many levels.

Consistency in developing your practice is important. You are forming a new beneficial habit, so pick a time and place that allows you to sit quietly every day, without interruption. Soon, just like the habit of stumbling out of bed and over to the coffeepot, you may start your meditation without thinking about it. To make it an integral part of your daily life, you want it to become automatic. Meditation takes practice, and for those who are impatient it can be especially beneficial.

Although meditation is, in essence, a universal practice, it is a different experience for everyone. Some ancient traditions may disagree, but if it does not work for you to meditate in the morning, try sitting quietly before dinner or take time out during your lunch hour. Meditation is an excellent way to switch gears, and if you need a transition after work, meditation is your key. There is something to the idea of "Happy Hour" — people naturally want to relax at that time of day, it is a transition time. Next time you feel like having a cocktail or a beer after work, try meditating as an alternative; it calms you down and can be very restorative. And it is free without the harmful side effects!

My mornings are often so packed and energetic that my meditations don't always take on the calm quality I am hoping for. Slowing down and sitting later in the day feels more relaxed and is a way to let go of the activities of the day. My personal experience is that meditating before dinner can sometimes feel "more potent," perhaps it is because I am less in the doing mode and more relaxed and receptive. Meditation before dinner is like a sigh of relief after the demands of the workday and it also improves your digestion, switching your nervous system into rest and digest mode.

Some people prefer to meditate before going to sleep at night, if you can stay awake! That time is nice for those whose families or careers make such demands on them that they may not have another chance during their hectic day. Finding quiet time alone at bedtime is a good way to wind down. There is something to be said about saying our prayers before going to sleep. The Judeo-Christian tradition teaches us to say our prayers at bedtime. Thinking good thoughts as we drift off to sleep can be effective for programming our minds to make positive changes in our lives and helps us sleep.

Our lives now are so fast paced and full, it can be difficult to go from working late or watching the news right to sleep. Having quiet time before bedtime is important to help us make the transition to restful sleep. Meditation before bedtime can program our dreams and set the tone for the next day. It can also wipe the slate clean (or cleaner) if you have had a stressful day. What you do before sleep can be deeply influential to your psyche. You may notice the difference between watching an action thriller before going to bed or reading an inspirational book. Personally, I could never watch the ten o'clock news and expect a good night's sleep. Watching any screen, such as your cell phone, computer or television can stimulate the brain and can be an obstacle to relaxation and sleep.

For chronic insomniacs and for night owls, the quiet hours in the middle of the night might be the perfect time to meditate. Sitting in the dark can be powerful and eliminates many sensory distractions. Many adults and children are afraid of the dark, especially those who have not spent much time in nature. When meditating alone in the dark, the only thing you can truly watch is your mind and its workings, including fear. Eliminating your fear of the dark may be an excellent way to build your personal power and develop confidence in all aspects of your life. Sitting with a candle is a good way to focus and can also train the mind. Make sure you don't fall asleep with the candle burning!

Ideally, meditation would be a daily activity, just like drinking coffee or tea in the morning. Please do not SHOULD yourself if you don't meditate every day and please don't make it another obligation on your to-do list. If you dip your toe in the cool, still waters of meditation only when you feel like it, that, at least is something!

My own personal experience is that meditation works best for me twice a day. For some, that would seem a luxury. Transcendental Meditation (TM) encourages practitioners to meditate for fifteen to twenty minutes twice a day, before breakfast and before dinner, no matter what. In Traditional Chinese medicine, the hours between 5:00 and 7:00 am or pm, or between 11:00 and 1:00—mid-day or midnight—are considered the best times to meditate.

In my own experience, for some reason, those times are conducive to practice. Try it for yourself.

Transcendental Meditation changed many lives in the 1960's and 70's when it first migrated out of India, and it probably continues to do so more quietly now in the 21st century. It was introduced to the Western world by Maharishi Mahesh Yogi and was a structured system easily adaptable for Westerners. A new meditator would be given meditation instructions and a personal mantra, or sacred sound, to repeat silently in meditation. The repetitive use of a mantra is an effective way to engage the brain and calm the body.

One of the reasons that Transcendental Meditation is so effective and successful is that students make a commitment to meditate twice a day. The key term is "no matter what." It is surprising how a positive habit can be so easy to maintain if it is given a front seat and a priority with the decision to meditate twice a day "no matter what." There is much to be said for having the support and reinforcement of a teacher or an established school of thought with its structure and protocol, a system that works, if you work it.

Some meditation traditions sit for forty minutes to an hour at a time, others twenty to twenty-five minutes. Recent research claims that 27 minutes is the optimal length of time for meditation. Start with less and don't strain yourself. You can always add more, after you begin to experience its benefits and if you are so inclined. If you set out to mediate for an hour as a beginner and discover that it is painful and that you have a lot to learn, you can get discouraged. Start small and as you become more comfortable with the process, you may begin to really enjoy it and may naturally feel like extending your practice.

I once meditated at a very traditional Buddhist monastery. The monks rose early and meditated for 90 minutes. On Sundays, they offered open meditation sessions for anyone who wanted to visit and would sit in silent meditation for 80 minutes. Oh my aching knees, that was a first for me, and very challenging! Prior to that the longest I had ever meditated in a group setting was 60 minutes at a Buddhist retreat center at 5:00am. Sometimes the teacher would fall asleep, which was agonizing for us visitors and some of the younger novice monks. Everyone was shifting in their seats, and would cough and clear their throats, hoping to wake up the leader, if it wasn't so uncomfortable, it would have been funny!

The importance of stillness cannot be overstated. It is taught in yoga and has been backed by neuroscience that it takes a good seven minutes for your body and mind to relax and settle down for the physiological effects to kick in. We live normally in the fight or flight mode of our sympathetic nervous system. After about seven minutes of silence and stillness, our bodies spontaneously shift to the parasympathetic nervous system, or the rest and digest mode. If you can manage to sit still for seven minutes, you may get past the bump of thinking too much and go on to sit for a longer period.

There are benefits to taking a few minutes to breathe and center during stressful times. If you manage five or ten minutes of meditation, or even one, that is good. In the yogic tradition, taking twelve deep, slow breaths is a common practice, both on and off the meditation seat. Remember, you are trying to create a habit of being calm. The more you do it, the better you get, the easier it is to return to that state and the longer you can stay. You can train yourself to relax when you need to be.

When you sit down to meditate, it takes a few minutes of stillness for the mind to settle and the muscles of the body to release. Some days are no doubt easier than others, sometimes you may feel that it is no use, you cannot sit still, your monkey mind won't be quiet — so maybe you give up. At those times take a break and don't give yourself a hard time if you don't stick it out. Try again later.

At those times when you stay with it and remain physically still and quiet, eventually your mind will usually become still and quiet as well. At some point you might think about making a commitment to sit for fifteen or twenty minutes, (no matter what!) and remember, it is called *practice;* and as you get familiar with the process, and you may find yourself making progress when you attend to it on a regular basis.

For some, sitting still may feel like a near impossibility! As stated earlier in the book, you might think of meditation as a workout, building muscle. Start with small, manageable increments. You might congratulate yourself for sitting for one whole minute the first time you succeed. As you begin, it is more important to practice regularly than it is to sit for long periods. Willing yourself to grit your teeth and power through 20 minutes of pain or discomfort is not our objective!

In the beginning, it may be helpful to have a timer, so you are not distracted with thoughts of wondering how much time has gone by or anticipating the end. I would avoid the old-fashioned timers that tick, as that can be very annoying! As you progress in your practice eventually you may not need or want a timer, and you may choose to extend the duration of your meditation. When using a timer, make a deal with yourself. Tell yourself to rest into stillness, don't move or say anything, don't look at the clock. Sit patiently for twenty minutes or however long the timer is set for. This is the one time of the day when self-absorption is a good thing!

Most cell phones have timers and alarms on them and there are many free meditation apps that offer timers for smart phones. When meditation apps first came out, I investigated them and was not impressed. After meditating for decades, I judged them as a distraction, a screen addiction for people who were not purists or traditionalists. Years later, as I was revisiting the basics of meditation, I decided to download a timer. I picked the most popular free one, *Insight Timer* and it gave me many happy surprises. First, I was stunned that there were tens of millions of users worldwide who use the app. The number continues to grow, and hundreds of thousands of users may be using it at one time. This is a new kind of worldwide community of meditators. It is a nice feeling, while meditating, to think about others that are meditating with you at that very moment. Whether you are connected by an electronic app, or just being on the same plane of consciousness, that feeling of unity is good to nurture.

So, to start, I set the timer and chose a simple, beautiful sound of a bell to begin and end the session. I was impressed by every aspect of the experience. My judgments abated the more my ignorance dissolved. The array of options on the app were vast; users could choose between guided meditations, instructional videos, beautiful music, and lectures from every tradition. I was shocked at what an amazing world was accessible, including courses in mindfulness, time management, overcoming depression and addiction, to name a few. I found myself enjoying the benefits of sonic healing, guided sleep aids and stress relief.

Later *Insight Timer* added live yoga classes and private sessions with teachers of all kinds. I ended up reviewing the app, calling it the greatest invention of the Aquarian Age (so far). Now, I would encourage anyone who has the desire and ability to try it or any of the others that are on the market that I don't have experience with. Most are free, and even if you use only the timer and don't explore the other options, it is a support to your practice.

Chapter Summary: When?

When to meditate:

1. Upon waking, first thing in the morning.
2. Before engaging in chatter, technology or watching the news.
3. Before breakfast, before getting too caffeinated.
4. Before dinner.
5. Before bedtime.
6. After hydrating; drink plenty of water!
7. In the TM tradition, twice a day, no matter what.
8. In Traditional Chinese medicine, the hours between 5:00 and 7:00 am or pm or between 11:00 and 1:00 —mid-day or midnight.
9. Transitioning from work, giving a new definition to Happy Hour!
10. When you are upset, sick, or recovering from injury or trauma.

Chapter 4

Where?

"Meditation must enter into every corner of our life."

—J. Krishnamurti

To the highly achieved meditation master the answer to "Where?" is anywhere and everywhere. For the rest of us, well... To integrate the daily practice of meditation into your life, it is important to have a quiet, solitary place that affords a sense of tranquility. For your meditation time, create a sanctuary to retreat to — for most of us that is our home. If you have a favorite room or corner in which to set up a meditation cushion or chair, find a time to have it all to yourself. If you follow a religion or spiritual tradition, you can meditate in front of your altar or picture or statue of your object of devotion.

If you have a friend, partner, or family member to meditate with, that is wonderful. You can share your meditation space with others — that is, if having company supports your practice. Sometimes it is easier to adopt an activity if we have a buddy; so, by all means, support each other in your practices. Meditation is the best way of getting to know yourself and your own mind. In many instances having others present, especially in the beginning, can be a distraction. Take the time to meditate on your own and do not wait for others.

The exception would be to find a meditation group and meet regularly with them. Groups offer a different quality of meditation and can be beneficial to the beginner and advanced meditator alike. Often, even experienced meditators might be surprised at the quality of meditation they experience in a group, especially with other longtime meditators. It's like hitch-hiking on someone else's elevated consciousness! If you have the opportunity to meditate with a great teacher or meditation master, please consider saying yes to that experience; you may find it interesting and maybe even life changing.

The bigger your city, the more options you have. You can search "Meditation" and be dazzled by the array of offerings. These can include counseling centers, AA programs, churches, Buddhist centers, and yoga studios. Even fitness clubs, community centers and colleges now offer meditation classes and ongoing groups, often free or very reasonable in cost. Hospitals generally have chapels, as do many rehab centers and clinics.

Some people may not have many options for places to meditate. Perhaps you have a disability or are struggling with poverty and can't afford a class or transportation. Or it may not be possible to have a meditation room or corner in your home. Any chair or quiet place in your house will do. For those who travel extensively or for those whose homes are not peaceful, and even for people who do not have a home at all, you can still meditate.

Some environments are naturally conducive to a meditative state. Any place of beauty, especially in nature, gardens, or parks, can be a good place to meditate. People (and animals) find peace sitting near water — be it the ocean, a fountain, or a moving stream. If you like to hike or camp, take time on the trail or at the campsite to sit and meditate. Visiting ancient temples or beautiful cathedrals, you may feel drawn to sit quietly and breathe in the atmosphere.

You can turn your car into a meditation chamber when needed, taking a break during a long drive, or if you arrive at your destination a few minutes early. You can retreat to your car for a lunch break meditation session during your workday. Some commuters meditate on the train or bus, which are good training grounds for staying focused. I know one traveler who had a profound life-changing meditation experience in the stall of an airport bathroom!

Chapter Summary: Where?

Where to meditate:

1. At home in any quiet, private place in your house.
2. If possible, designate a special place specifically for meditation.
3. If you are religious, in front of your altar.
4. In nature, especially by water – ocean, river, ponds, fountains.
5. In a parked car, before leaving or after reaching the destination or to take a break during a long drive.
6. While traveling, in planes, trains or buses.
7. In a church, temple, or sacred space.
8. In a meditation group or yoga center.
9. In the hospital or rehabilitation center.
10. In jail or prison.

Chapter 5

Why?

"The ultimate reason for meditating is to transform ourselves in order to be better able to transform the world."

—Matthieu Ricard

When you start researching the benefits of meditation, what you find can be astonishing. It is hard to pick up a current magazine without finding an article about mindfulness or insight meditation by a wellness expert, often with the endorsement of a celebrity, about why meditation is so great.

Clinical trials have been conducted at least since the 1950's, and possibly earlier, on the effects of meditation on the mind and body and even on society. Now even the most prestigious institutions are taking the subject seriously and conducting their own research. There is a growing body of medical evidence that concludes that meditation is a most beneficial therapy. The National Institutes of Health, UCLA, the Mayo Clinic, Johns Hopkins University, Harvard Medical School, M.D. Anderson Cancer Center and the University of Wisconsin are just a few of the research facilities that are finding that people who meditate are physiologically and psychologically different than those who do not.

Much of the early research done in the United States was conducted specifically on Transcendental Meditation (TM) while clinical trials in Japan have focused on Zen meditation. When Buddhism spread to Japan, it merged with the local Samurai culture and grew to be what we now call Zen. Neuroscience and the medical field lead the research today in what is known as *mindfulness-based* or *insight meditation*. The Buddhist term is *Vipassana*.

Research claims that 80 to 90 percent of illnesses are caused by stress. A small percentage of illness is genetic. Disease caused by toxins and other environmental factors are more threatening if our immune systems are stressed or compromised. Cortisol is known as the stress hormone and is released by the adrenal glands in response to perceived threatening situations. In small doses it elevates the blood sugar levels, energizing the body to fuel the fight or flight response. When you experience prolonged or chronic stress, negative health outcomes are much more likely. Think of chronic stress as being Cortisol Poisoning, which can affect all our body systems.

Meditation increases activity in the part of the brain associated with positive mental states. For this reason, therapists suggest meditation for relief of depression and anxiety disorders. Medical doctors not only prescribe it, in some cases they even teach it to their patients.

There is a strong link between calm states of mind and increased immune function as well as lowered blood pressure, slower heartbeat, and heightened brain activity. Meditation is proving to help veterans cope with post-traumatic stress disorder (PTSD), and young people are making improvements in hyperactivity disorders and emotional instability through meditation. Recent studies have discovered that meditation can even change and regenerate our DNA!

One of the early claims from TM research is that meditation promotes longevity. They asserted that if someone has been practicing TM regularly for fifteen years or more, their biological age is an average of twelve years younger than their chronological age. In other words, if you are sixty years old and have been meditating for fifteen years, you have the physiology of a forty-eight-year-old. Although this would be difficult to quantify, who wouldn't want it?

People who meditate tend to instinctively make positive changes in their lifestyles, such as increasing body awareness, beginning an exercise regimen, adopting a healthier diet, changing sleep habits, and letting go of destructive tendencies, including abandoning abusive habits and toxic relationships.

Many years ago, I read that if one percent of the population meditates "effectively," it can reduce the violent crime rate by over 20 percent. It makes sense that if more people can find inner peace, world peace will follow. I heard this statistic many years ago and it resonated with me, long before I decided to write this book. I wish now I had made a note of the source of this information!

In 1976, the Office of the Assistant Secretary of Defense approved a Pentagon Meditation Club. It eventually had over 17,000 members in the U.S. Defense Department, holding weekly peace meditations. The organization launched what they called the SDI, or Spiritual Defense Initiative. It is interesting that even the U.S. Department of Defense once sanctioned meditation as a beneficial practice. I hate to imagine how history may have been different, had not these conscious individuals taken a stand for peace.

Similarly, the United Nations works with hundreds of non-governmental organizations (NGOs) with consultative status to further the cause of global peace. Groups such as Lucis Trust and World Goodwill have supported the UN through meditation, educational materials and seminars, reaching millions of individuals and hundreds of countries around the world.

Chapter Summary: Why?

Why Meditate:

1. Improves health.
2. Promotes longevity.
3. Regenerates DNA.
4. Lowers blood pressure.
5. Stabilizes emotions.
6. Improves memory and brain function.
7. Improves sleep.
8. Increases awareness, intuition.
9. Reduces anger and violent crime.
10. Promotes inner peace and world peace.

Chapter 6

How?

"The mind is like a glass of muddy water. When the glass is still, the mud settles, and the water eventually becomes clear. So it is with the mind. If you sit still, eventually your obscurations dissolve and the mind becomes clear."

—*The Venerable Lama Karma Rinchen*

Meditation systems are based on principles that are important to observe. There are seven basic traditional guidelines to begin a meditation practice: sitting, posture, shoulders and arms, hands, neck and chin, eyes and mouth. You can go through the checklist at the back of the book every time you meditate to remind you of the key points until it becomes second nature.

1. Sitting

My original Taoist master said to sit regally, like a king or queen on a throne, with an attitude of relaxed formality and dignity. Meditation can be practiced sitting on a cushion, chair, bench, or bed.

Sit where you are comfortable, where you can have good posture and can remain still throughout the duration of the practice.

For those with back injuries, or other conditions which do not allow prolonged sitting, meditation can be done lying down. Make sure your body is aligned and centered. Having a cushion, rolled towel or blanket under your knees is helpful for your lower back. Please place a small pillow, cushion or folded blanket under your head so that your forehead is slightly higher than your chin to lengthen the back of your neck. It is more challenging to stay awake laying down, so you may want to meditate when you are not tired.

If you are sitting in a chair, have both feet flat on the floor or if your feet do not reach the floor, rest them on a stool, cushion or folded blanket. You do not need to sit back in the chair. If you do, it is important for good posture to have lumbar support. You can use a small pillow or a folded towel at your lower back or you can use a lumbar support cushion often sold for driving. Do not lean sideways or cross your legs at the knees or ankles when sitting in a chair. Try to remain as centered and symmetrical as possible.

If you meditate on the floor and are physically able, sitting cross-legged on a cushion is great. Make sure your knees are not higher than your hips. If they are, add height to your seat. Many people cannot sit cross-legged but they can sit comfortably on their knees, legs folded under, Japanese style. However you sit on the floor, a meditation cushion, firm pillow, or folded blanket to elevate the hips is very helpful. This helps us sit up straight, can ease discomfort in the legs and hips and helps keep your posture upright.

Yogis often sit in a full or half lotus position, which is excellent for meditation. This requires hip flexibility and is not always possible for those who grew up in the West. Most Westerners spend their lives on chairs and sofas, and either cannot sit on the floor or would be so uncomfortable that it would distract from meditation. So, begin your practice as simply and as comfortably as possible.

Another excellent way to meditate, for those not comfortable on the floor – is to perch on the edge of a chair, bed, or large exercise ball. This is a Taoist method that works for some people who for various reasons cannot do sitting meditation in other positions. When you perch on the very edge of a chair, your spine is erect and your legs are level or below your seat, with your groin area open. You are resting on your sitting bones. This makes it easy to sit upright with your shoulders back and your chest open. This is also a good sitting position while working at a desk or computer and can prevent pain in your back, hips, neck or shoulders.

2. Posture

Having your spine gently erect is important and is the natural tendency of the body. Good posture is essential to full breathing, proper meditation, and good health. When you sit, lengthen the distance from your crotch to your rib cage and lift your heart (literally and poetically!). This lengthens the spine, moves your shoulders back, opens your chest, and allows for deep, full relaxed breathing. You may notice immediately how much more alive you feel when you are open and breathing fully. Physical therapists use a descriptive phrase to describe the lengthening of the spine: strive for "maximum vertebral axial extension." Try saying that ten times quickly!

I like to imagine a thread pulling the tailbone down and anchoring my body solidly into the earth. I imagine roots growing down out of my pelvic root. Sensing the ground, gravity and a solid base is a good way to start your practice. In the same way, imagine a thread pulling the crown of the head upwards. You may notice that this immediately lifts you up and lengthens the spine. You can even pull gently on your hair at your crown, you may notice your body immediately reacting by getting taller. Whenever you meditate your muscle memory may remind you what it feels like to pull up on your hair anytime you need to straighten up!

The physical hatha yoga that most of us know was developed thousands of years ago by meditators to enhance their meditation experience. Sri T. Krishnamacharya, widely considered the father of modern yoga, was asked how much yoga practice one should do. He replied that essentially, enough yoga to enable one to sit comfortably in meditation. Some yogis say there is really only one yoga posture and that is sitting cross-legged on the floor; that all other *asana* or yoga positions are training vehicles to stay comfortably in the sitting position for extended periods. The literal translation of asana is "to sit upright." In the Western world, it is generally translated as posture.

There are many yoga poses with slight backbend type movement that help open the chest and shoulders. Sitting in one position can be a strain on the body; so much of our lives are spent at a desk, behind the wheel of a car or on a sofa. It is imperative to balance and move the body. If you feel like you have been stuck in one position too long, give your loyal body a break, it is always there doing what you tell it to do. Try doing what your body asks you to do for a change! Move those areas that scream at you when you have been sitting too long. As you develop your awareness and learn to listen to your body, you can hear it when it starts whispering. Please pay attention and give it what it asks for before it has to raise its voice!

Once the posture is set, there is no reason to move, remain in stillness and rest into the moment. One moment after the other. The foundation on which meditation rests and from which meditative experience arises is stillness of body and mind. Stilling the mind is influenced by stillness of body and correctness of posture.

3. Shoulders and Arms

Shoulders are aligned above your hips and below your ears. We can consciously move our shoulders slightly back and relax them down. As you do this, remember to tuck your chin, as we may naturally stick out neck out when rolling our shoulders back. The elbows are gently pointed out away from the body; the arms are not flat against your sides but rather the armpits are slightly open for circulation.

If you find that tight shoulders restrict your breathing, try to practice opening your chest when you are off the cushion and see how your posture improves. While you are walking, you can lead with your pelvis, lift your heart, and swing your arms. This re-trains your chest and shoulders to relax into the open position.

4. Hands

For now, the position of your hands depends on what feels comfortable to you. Your hands may be folded on your lap or rested on your thighs, palms up or down. Some traditions use specific hand mudras. There are many ways of holding the hands and fingers that are symbolic, often for energetic or healing purposes. For example, in the yogic tradition meditators are often depicted holding the palms up with the thumb and index finger touching, forming a circle, while the other three fingers are straight. Many Buddhists rest the hands below the navel, palms up, one on top of the other with the thumbs lightly touching. I like meditating in this position; you can imagine that your upturned, open palms are gently holding the world. However you choose to hold your hands, it is important that they are relaxed, and they do not reach forward, pulling your shoulders down.

5. Neck and chin

The neck and jaw are relaxed, and the head rests naturally and loosely at the top of the spine. The head should feel as if it were suspended from the crown. The position of your neck is held tall while lightly tilting the chin downward and gently bringing it inward. Do not hold your chin up or jut it forward. You can tuck it in gently, keeping your neck relaxed. Think of your head gently bowing to your heart.

On or off the meditation seat, always correct your posture if you find your head jutting forward. This "forward head position" is a condition often occurring in people who slouch on the sofa, spend a lot of time driving or in front of a computer. It is a subtle and under-recognized condition, which left uncorrected, causes all manner of problems, not just in the neck and shoulders, but all through the body. Your head is very heavy and when it is in front of your body, your neck and shoulders tighten up, it is very hard on the neck. In this position, it is difficult to hold your head up, leading to headaches and structural problems. It signals a stress condition to the body, which triggers anxiety. This can age us! Entire books are written about the importance of good posture, not just in meditation but for health and well-being. When you are sitting in meditation, it is essential to find a position that you can sustain without slumping. Always be aware of how your head sits on your neck. Remember when we were young and our parents and teachers told us to sit up straight? They were right!

6. Eyes

Meditation may be done with your eyes closed or slightly open. When you close your eyes, the left side of your brain, the analytical side, slows down and your right side is activated, engaging your parasympathetic nervous system. For beginners, it may be easier to lightly close your eyes; in this way, you have less visual distraction, can relax and more closely observe the inner workings of your body and mind.

If you prefer to meditate with your eyes open, rest your gaze a few inches from the tip of your nose or at a spot on the floor that is not moving; soften your gaze so you are looking at nothing in particular. Your gaze is relaxed and does not wander. Meditating with your eyes open is good training for coping with distractions and carrying the meditative state into every aspect of your everyday life. Because of fear or trauma, some people do not feel safe closing their eyes. If we do not feel safe in our environment, it is difficult to release our attention from it.

If you practice Buddhism, or are interested in exploring Buddhist meditation, you may want to initially begin meditating with your eyes open. A Buddhist teacher once told me, "Closed eyes, closed mind!" If you have already formed a habit of meditating with the eyes closed and then try to meditate with them open, it can be challenging. Making the change to meditating with eyes open after years, or even decades, is not easy to do. If you have a hard time meditating with the eyes open, meditating in the dark can be a good practice.

The Inner Smile

From the Taoist tradition, you may like to adopt the technique of the inner smile. Practice smiling with your eyes as well as your mouth. When you settle down to meditate and scan your body to make sure you are relaxed, consciously adopt the feeling of smiling with your eyes. This is a subtle and powerful way to get a smiling, happy feeling inside your whole body. This is a practice which greatly affects your vagus nerve, having a positive affect on your entire nervous system. You can practice smiling at your heart or other internal organs or body parts and extend this smiling feeling to every cell in your body. This can set the tone for a very nice meditation session and can be a gentle healing practice in itself. You may have met and have been touched by individuals who have smiling eyes: the Dalai Lama is probably the most recognizable example. Many people have naturally smiling eyes and it is also something you can do intentionally — it is easy to learn.

7. Mouth

The mouth and face are relaxed, and the teeth and jaws are not clenched. The tip of the tongue rests on the roof of your mouth, behind your upper teeth. The lips are lightly touching while your upper and lower teeth are apart. If your mouth is tightly closed, it is very easy to tense your mouth, lips, or jaw, so please consciously relax your entire face. Having your teeth together brings tension to the mouth and jaw. Some yoga teachers say there is no reason for your upper and lower teeth to touch if you are not chewing. Some traditions teach that the lips are mostly closed, with just an open space the size of a kernel of rice at the center point. It is nice to begin your meditation with the corners of your mouth lifted in a slight, gentle smile, as long as your mouth is relaxed.

Now that you are sitting with intention, watch your breath.

Take a deep breath and exhale slowly. You can now focus your attention on your breath, observing it without trying to control it. Watch it go in and out, much like sitting on the beach watching the waves. First focus on the breath as it comes in and out the tip of the nostrils. This is the point where the air becomes breath. Notice the quality of your breathing. Feel the coolness on your nostrils as the air goes in and becomes your breath. Feel the warm breath as it comes out and becomes the air once more.

You can follow your breath as it goes into your lower lungs, middle lungs, and upper lungs. As you breathe into your navel area allow your belly and ribcage to expand lightly and contract as you exhale. In this way, your breath can reach the lower lung area. Most of us have shallow breathing, filling only the upper and middle area of the lungs. If you have good posture, your breathing can be much fuller.

Maintain the focus on the breath. Thoughts naturally arise. When a thought distracts you, gently return your attention to the breath. Other thoughts will arise. Pay attention to the process in your mind without getting caught up in it. Gently return to your breath. As a thought comes, let it dissolve and try not to follow it with another thought. Always gently return to your breath. It doesn't matter what your thoughts are; don't engage with them. Don't believe everything you think! And don't give yourself a hard time for thinking or for not focusing—just passively observe the breath.

In observing the breath, we are switching our awareness from thoughts in our minds to sensations in our bodies. While focusing on your breath, be aware of how it feels. As you become aware of the sensation of the breath going in and out of your nostrils, the feeling of the breath as it fills your lungs, or the difference in how your head and awareness feel, you may find yourself less concerned with your thoughts. We are turning our attention from thinking and doing to feeling and being.

For some people, meditation's goal is to turn off one's thoughts completely — good luck with that! Meditation, as we are describing it in this book, is also about observing our thoughts to better understand the nature of one's mind. With practice, the mind becomes quieter and more stable.

People are generally not aware that their minds are constantly engaged in activity, the Monkey Mind. That one becomes aware of the constant chatter in the mind is a sign of progress. When you attempt to still the mind, you become aware of how chaotic it is.

The air we breathe and our awareness of it is the bridge that connects the body with the outside world. The breath unifies the outer world with the inner world. With continued practice, there is no separation between the two. You may sit down to meditate one day and suddenly realize that you had a brief period with no thoughts. You may recognize that something was very different and think that wow, that was something! Sometimes referred to as the gap, it is a definite departure from our normal waking consciousness.

With continued practice you may find yourself to be more tolerant, less judgmental and more open to conditions that may have once bothered you. By cultivating this feeling of oneness, you may learn to navigate the realm of duality and judgments of right and wrong or likes or dislikes. It's all good, in 21st century parlance.

The breath is like a swinging pendulum between the extremes of in and out and full and empty. The inhale leads to expansion, awareness and maybe even bliss. The exhale teaches us to let go, release, and relax, the key to liberation. As you observe your breath, become aware of the subtle nuances of your awareness. Are you more focused on the inhale or the exhale? Do you notice the gaps between the inhale and the exhale? Do you notice if your inhale is longer than your exhale or vice versa?

The breath is the portal into a realm beyond thought. Breath, stillness, and relaxation are the three foundations of meditation practice. In those fleeting moments between thoughts, you may become aware of the peaceful state of emptiness that is unsullied by concepts, thoughts, and ideas. As your practice deepens, you may find that these gaps in thinking become more frequent with longer duration. Follow the breath and it may lead you into the ground of being where pure awareness abides.

Calm Abiding

For basic meditation Tibetans use the word *shamatha* or *samatta*, which means *calm abiding*. Descriptive and simple. I love this name, sometimes just thinking the words calm abiding might channel inner stillness! In this case, to abide means to stay in one place. So, our mind's attention is not allowed to wander, but simply abides calmly in one place. Another way to describe it is to simply "be." When you sit quietly, observing your breath, you are just being, nothing else. Observe what it feels like to rest in beingness, right here, right now and remember, we are human beings, not human doings. Some would say that we are both. Just make sure that we give as much attention to being and feeling as we do thinking and doing, which has its place, but not on the meditation seat!

I love this passage from Tibetan teacher, Khentin Tai Situ Rinpoche about *samatta*:

"The first aspect of meditation is the development of an inner awareness that acquaints one with the mind as it really is, beneath its superficial layer of obscuration. When there is no practice of meditation it is impossible to practice generosity, skillful conduct, forbearance and diligence fully - they cannot become 'perfections' because their very essence, this inner awareness is lacking. In order to get to know our mind as it is, we first practice *samatta* (Tib. *shi-nay*) meditation. This makes the mind more tranquil and lets it rest in its own qualities, free from the disturbing presence of recent accumulations. Samatta is developed by cultivating an awareness, a mindfulness of everything that arises. In the meditation session we relax the body, speech and mind and rest naturally and simply in the present state which is by nature free from all the obstacle-delusions of desire, anger, ignorance, jealousy and pride."

Mental Notes

Some mindfulness methods suggest labeling what comes up in meditation. For example, you start focusing on the breath, noting the inbreath as "inhale" and the outbreath, "exhale." Or "I am breathing in... I am breathing out." So, you sit for a bit and are distracted by a siren or the honking of a horn. Note it as "noise" or "traffic." Here too, don't pay much attention to it, just note it, and return your attention to the breath. Whatever distracts you, you don't need to engage with it or identify or analyze it, just let it go.

You may find yourself dwelling on an itch; see if you can note it as "itch" or "sensation" and let go of any power it has over you and watch it dissolve into nothingness. You might even smile at them, itches can be funny!

Having an itch is a wonderful meditation tool. For the most part, itches are harmless and fleeting. Meet them with curiosity and interest, and see if you might stay neutral, not judging them bad or annoying. See if you can keep still and not tense up. When you study the actual nature of your mind through meditation, you might notice that the itch is a sensation, that's all. It is impermanent and inconsequential. You have heard the term, "What you resist, persists"? If you try to resist the itch and force yourself to ignore it and rigidly power through, it can cause tension and be a distraction. And, of course, the itch will persist. If you objectively examine the itch, momentarily put your attention on it, breathe into it and accept it, the itch loses its power over you. Like the thoughts that arise in your meditation, the itch will also dissolve. Just breathe into it and watch it dissipate and go back to the breath.

Much the same can be said of pain. For people in pain, meditation can be an effective coping mechanism. If you breathe into the pain, you might notice that it makes a difference in how you experience it. When you accept the pain, rather than resist it, without labeling it as "bad" or unpleasant, the pain itself can subside, or at least, take on a different quality. There is a very real distinction between pain and suffering. Resisting the pain makes it worse, brings up judgment and aversion and turns your experience into one of suffering. When pain arises, view it objectively, like you would your breath, accept it as a sensation. Pain is a phenomenon that too many people live with, and meditation can be helpful in coming to grips with it. Of course, if the pain while you meditate is related to extreme discomfort from your seat or posture, by all means, do something about it!

Sensations as they arise will come and go. Please pay attention to pain or discomfort. You might make a mental note, "pain" or "discomfort," and try to bring your awareness back to the breath. Keep in mind that pain and discomfort are real and tend to persist; when they arise, tend to it, take a breath, take a break, maybe all you need is to reposition yourself. Or perhaps in your receptive state you have become aware of a condition you were not previously aware of. Whatever your body is asking for, please co-operate. Don't take it personally; don't feel bad or give yourself a hard time, there is no value in rigidly sitting through what can go past mere annoyance into actually hurting your body. It can be defeating and cause harm. This is self-care coming to the meditation seat.

Counting the Breaths

For those beginning your exploration into meditation, counting the breaths can be helpful, as opposed to simply observing them. This method engages both sides of the brain and can be easier for some people to stay focused. If you are counting your breaths, there is less room for thoughts to invade. As you calmly watch your breath, count each inhale and exhale as one breath. The next inhale and exhale would be two, continue up to twenty-one or whatever number you choose. Getting distracted after just a few breaths is common; when that happens, start over with one. If a beginner succeeds in reaching twenty-one, they are doing exceptionally well. If you make it to twenty-one, then on the next breath start again with one and continue the process. Again, if thoughts arise, do not hold on. Let them go and gently return to counting the breath. I have found that this is a good introduction to quieting your mind; you may suddenly realize that the counting has naturally fallen away, and time has passed in a peaceful meditative state.

Counting the breaths can come in handy anytime. For mini meditations during the day, if you find yourself distressed, anxious, angry, or impatient, try taking 12 deep, slow breaths and see what happens. If you try this when you become stressed out while driving, please remember to keep your eyes open!

Mantra

You can also engage the use of mantra, or sacred sound, to focus on. This is a widespread practice that is taught in many traditions. It is especially helpful for people who are auditory learners. As you settle into meditation, silently say a sound that is meaningful to you while coordinating it with the inhale and the exhale. A good one is "Om," or "Aum," said to be the primordial sound of the universe.

Start by taking a deep breath in and, on the exhale, let out a long syllable, whichever you choose, that matches the length of your exhale. If you go with the classic "Om," it is mostly an open "oh" sound, ending with the mmm sound at the end, with a little pause afterward as you inhale. Try this aloud as a toning, quieting and centering exercise for a minute or two.

When you begin your meditation, you can practice by saying the mantra aloud and continue to make the sound quieter and softer, until you are repeating the sound silently, internally. Settle in with the rhythm of the sound. The same rules apply regarding distractions; if you find yourself thinking about your shopping list or what you are going to have for dinner, gently return to the sound. Eventually you may find that your mind stays busy with the sound and thoughts find it harder to intrude. The sound can lead you to a very open transcendent state.

If you resonate with the Judeo-Christian tradition, a good mantra with Old Testament roots is, "I am that I am," the translation of which has been a question for the ages. It is said as a continuous sound loop, without beginning or end, the length of your breath, "I am that I am that I am that I am that I am that I am that I am that I am that I am..." You can whisper or repeat the sound silently on the inbreath if you wish.

After a while you might realize that you are no longer focusing on the breath or your mantra. They are steps that lead you up a ladder of consciousness, and you may find yourself resting in pure awareness. What does that mean, exactly? The best answer is to practice meditation and then try to describe it yourself!

When you focus on the breath or a mantra, remember to put your attention on the sensation of the breath, the physical experience in your body. When you note the inhale and the exhale or the words of a mantra, those are concepts that you can be aware of and immediately let them go. Our goal is to eventually release thoughts or concepts about the experience and to be with the experience itself.

As you progress you may find yourself being fascinated with the breath, mantra and the meditation experience itself. Time can go by quickly and you may be inspired to sit for longer periods. At times, you may also think of your practice as a series of "shorties"; in other words, if you meditate for five minutes and get distracted, you can take a deep breath and go into it again. You may meditate for a few minutes and realize you are painfully uncomfortable, and you need to reposition yourself. Go ahead, start over. As you continue to practice you learn how to "find your seat," and are able to sit without moving for the entire session. And if you aren't able or it takes years, be okay with it.

Return to your breath, keep the mind still, and when thoughts arise, simply let them go. If you experience one or two minutes of "real" meditative absorption, you are making progress. Even if your mind is still full of thoughts, the process has its benefits, such as relieving stress. Especially in the West there is a tendency to value quantity over quality; that is, if something is small, it must be less important. Let go of that idea and appreciate a short meditation as being significant. Practice meditating every day.

How to end your meditation

In meditation you enter into a different state of consciousness, so be gradual in your return to everyday awareness. It can be a shock to come out of a meditative state suddenly. It is not uncommon for people to get a headache or other anxiety reaction from ending their meditation in a disturbing way. If you set an alarm to end the meditation, make sure it is a pleasant sound, like a gong or bell and not something "alarming" that may rattle your nervous system, undoing any calming benefits you may have experienced. When your meditation is over, you might follow the bell or gong into silence, just as you may have followed it into silence at the beginning. With the sound comes bringing your awareness back to your senses, your body, the room, the world. Don't rush to open your eyes; you might flutter them open slowly, especially in bright light situations. Wiggle your toes and fingers; you may want to stretch your neck or back. You don't want to undo meditation's positive effects!

When I finish meditating, I sometimes bring my palm to rest on my navel and cover it with my other palm. This has a grounding effect and brings you back "into your body" and can prevent you from feeling spacy.

Chapter Summary: How?

How to meditate:

1. Sit with an attitude of relaxed formality and dignity.
2. Good posture, with spine gently erect, be symmetrical.
3. Shoulders are aligned above your hips and below your ears.
4. Hands can be folded in your lap or resting on your thighs, facing up or down.
5. Neck is relaxed, head rests naturally at the top of the spin.
6. Chin is tucked in slightly.
7. Eyes can be closed or relaxed slightly open, gazing ahead of you at nothing in particular.
8. Mouth is relaxed, usually closed or with lips slightly parted.
9. The tongue rests at top of the palate, behind the upper front teeth.
10. Observe your breath or count the breaths.
11. Can make mental notes and return to focusing on the breath.
12. Can repeat a mantra, or sacred sound.

Chapter 7

And Then...

"**Letting go of control is the ultimate challenge for the spiritual warrior...**"

—*Chögyum Trungpa Rinpoche*

What can you expect from continued practice? While it may take time to notice changes in your meditation sessions, your mind and consciousness make subtle adjustments. You might notice more ease and calm during and after your practice and may notice subtle changes in your everyday awareness. Your mind's processes change in ways that may not be immediately apparent. And you may not even notice it yourself. Others may point out that you seem more calm, focused or even how good you look!

One student, whom I call Jenny, had chronic anxiety and childhood trauma and it was almost impossible for her to relax. She read about different types of meditation and felt like it was just what she needed. She understood it on an intellectual level. Her problem was with internalizing the process. She came to her meditation group regularly; she loved the group process and the feeling of quiet sitting; she just couldn't bring herself to meditate on her own at home. As Jenny became familiar with meditating in a group, she came to realize that she had a fear of being alone. The idea of sitting alone with herself was terrifying. Just becoming aware of this fear gave her insight into many of her problems, not just with meditation, but with her health, her relationships and even her problems at work.

When Jenny finally sat down to meditate at home, she would hold tightly to the process of being with her breath. The breath was her anchor, and she was afraid of not having something to cling to. Although she felt like she was not "good at meditating," the daily activity of sitting was helpful for her to calm her mind and body, and her health improved almost immediately.

The changes were subtle, and she did not even notice them for a long time. Like most people and Westerners in particular, Jenny sensed she was not "getting anywhere," as she put it. She understood that the process was helping, and she had read so much about meditation that she had high expectations. She kept at it and one day realized that she had made significant progress. After what seemed like years of diligent sitting, she had an observation that was very helpful for her. I am sharing it here because it illustrates a meditation process that I too have experienced, and she described very well.

Jenny experienced her breathing as being like a ladder or a staircase––very much a vertical ascent. With each breath, she climbed higher and with each step she felt she was leaving her physical problems and the cares of the material world behind her––or below her. At a certain point, she realized that she was not clinging so tightly to her breath, that she was not thinking of her breath or anything at all. The breath had delivered her through a threshold into a natural state of bliss, unrelated to thoughts or concepts, a very peaceful place to be.

Although it is important not to enter the practice of meditation with unrealistic expectations, it is also important to understand that it can have profound implications for the serious and committed practitioner.

Attention to your breath is the doorway to a different state of mind. After practicing for a while, a meditator may notice that after a few minutes that he or she is not focusing on the breath but is experiencing a type of calm emptiness, joy or even bliss. It is often characterized by light or feelings of illumination or realization. At that point, you have naturally let go of your attention to breathing. Allow the focus on the body and breathing to fade away and enjoy the sensation that breathing has led you to. Attention on the breath is the key to the doorway and once that doorway is opened, we no longer need the key.

Speaking of keys, once that door is unlocked, lock your attention onto the feeling of light and joy and meditate on that, while attention to the physical realm subsides. Keep your attention on the sensations, the emotion, swim in it! Experience the feeling of happiness and joy, without clinging. Don't think about it, judge it, or try to make it last longer. Your attention may relax into a comfortable feeling of contentment. Focus on that feeling, get used to it and remember what it feels like. Contentment is a wonderful quality to bring into your everyday consciousness — a good mental habit!

As you focus on the feeling of contentment, it may take on other qualities, like stillness, equanimity, or neutrality. All is good... Complete relaxation gives way to a grounded, secure feeling, allow this feeling of gravity, just relax into it. Think of this as the ground of your being and dwell in it. You may ask, what does this mean? What is described as the ground of our being, pure awareness are ways that people have tried to describe bliss, enlightenment of their experience of God or a Higher Power. Many cultures and languages around the world have words for attempting to describe these states. Whatever we choose to call it can be a controversial term, there are many names or terms that are used for whatever cannot be explained or controlled.

Meditation does not MAKE us healthy or happy or peaceful, we simply discover or realize these qualities, which are inherent in our natural state. This is the part where semantics, as well as philosophy, becomes irrelevant. The Bible references this path, goal and achievement as the ineffable, what cannot be described, spoken, or uttered. The world of the Spirit goes beyond the physical, of which words are a part. There comes a point in our consciousness where it is impossible to define or describe what we experience. The ancient Chinese use the word Tao, often translated as the way, or the path, but as Lao Tzu, the ancient Taoist, said, "The Tao that can be spoken, is not the true Tao."

Whatever your experience or understanding of God, Spirit, Higher Power, or inner self, what you call it is not important. If you trust it, if it feels right and leaves you feeling more balanced, happy, healthy, and spacious, it is leading you to the right place. The realization of coming to understand the nature of this ineffable state is a great benefit of our efforts.

In meditation one may experience feelings of spaciousness, which is associated with good moods and happiness. For most of us it is a quality that is far too infrequent. The more you experience this feeling of openness, the easier it is to return to it. Thinking good thoughts, feeling happy, smiling, and being in a good mood are all choices we make and good habits to cultivate. You may surprise yourself one day by realizing, "Hey, I am happy!"

I like the term, "from states to traits." If any emotional state, be it worry, fear, anger, or happiness, becomes chronic, it eventually becomes part of who you are, a character trait. If I say I am worried, eventually I may be described as a worrier. States of anger eventually create an angry person. The same is true of positive emotions. The more we experience security, happiness, or optimism as a fleeting state, it can become an ongoing emotional habit, a character trait. What a positive outcome and reason enough to meditate!

It is important to pay attention to whatever arises, mindfully being aware of unwelcome triggers or memories and not thoughtlessly react to them. Perhaps you can bring a sense of curiosity to whatever sensations come up and be intentional about your responses. Give yourself permission to pause, breathe, and feel relief. Breathe into the feelings mindfully, rather than meet them with avoidance and thoughtless reaction. Give yourself permission to make a shift, this is the practice.

Research has shown that with continued meditation our conscious mind can expand to include more and more of the unconscious and subconscious realms of the mind — as well as the superconscious.

As your practice deepens, as you more easily soften into surrender, the mental shields that armor you from uncomfortable issues may dissolve. You let your guard down. You may find that emotions, memories, uncomfortable sensations and even long held trauma arise. This could happen anytime, especially when you least expect it! For example, painful experiences from your childhood that you preferred not to think about have always been there, lodged in your body and mind. Perhaps these unconscious blockages to your happiness no longer serve you, no matter how hard you have unconsciously tried to suppress them. Then suddenly, they burst onto the scene of your conscious mind, no longer hiding in the darkness like a scary monster. They only arise when you are ready.

Rather than push these uncomfortable feelings away, you might view them as an opportunity to bring issues to the light of day and face them head on. Say good-bye, let them go and you might even thank them for whatever they did to serve you. Bringing them out of the shadows make them much less scary, making it be possible to see them for what they are. Your mindfulness practice may help you face uncomfortable stimuli objectively, devoid of the story or layers that have built up around them. Our conscious or unconscious stories about painful events tend to add layers of complexity to what might be a simple resolution. You may feel a breath of relief and feel lighter.

Chapter Summary: And Then...

And then what happens:

1. You may notice your mind making subtle adjustments.
2. You may notice more ease and calm.
3. You may become aware of fears and other subconscious patterns.
4. You may begin to experience insight into the nature of your problems.
5. Your health improves.
6. You may naturally let go of toxic habits or relationships.
7. You may discover your true, natural state of pure awareness, experiencing more happiness and joy.
8. It may become easier to detach from the material world and its entanglements.
9. You may come to understand that some experiences truly cannot be described or explained with words.
10. You may begin to embody positive states that lead to positive traits.

Chapter 8

Frequently Asked Questions

"If you are depressed, you are living in the past. If you are anxious, you are living in the future. If you are at peace, you are living in the present."

—*Lao Tzu*

I get so sleepy when I meditate, what can I do?

The most obvious cause of sleepiness is trying to meditate when you are tired or after a big meal. What time of day are you meditating? Are you getting enough sleep? The best time to meditate is after you awaken naturally, feeling refreshed. Poor posture or slumping forward is also a culprit of drowsiness, because your breath is restricted.

If you meditate with your eyes closed, try keeping them half open, following the directions in the "HOW" chapter. Also, position your arms so they are away from your body, making space around your armpits; this too may prevent drowsiness. Giving slightly more emphasis to your inhalation can energize you. To keep from falling asleep, try extending the length of the inhalation slightly, without forcing it. If it is early in the morning and you are still tired, if you are accustomed to drinking tea or coffee, have a cup before you meditate. Do not get so caffeinated that you can't sit still!

Also, if the room is too warm or if you have heavy clothes on, that can make your mind dull and drowsy. It's tricky; when we relax, meditate, or sleep, our body temperature naturally goes down, so then we might get too cold, which is also a distraction. There are many subtleties in our mind and body to become aware of, and as we spend more time meditating, we learn what works. Again, it is called *practice* for a reason!

I get home from work and want to meditate, but I am just so revved up, I can't turn my mind off. What do you suggest?

The practice of hatha yoga developed to help ancient yogis meditate better and sit longer. Physical exercise has a restorative effect on the body. If you have the time and opportunity to run, walk, swim, go to the gym or do yoga, to help you rest and unwind, go for it. It is wonderful that you are meditating after work. Meditation helps with managing stress, and it is a great way to celebrate "happy hour" as a transition time from your workday to your evening.

When you sit, leaning backward may cause your mind to be overactive and agitated, so first try to lean forward just a bit — it is a subtle shift. You want to keep your posture upright and find the right balance in your sitting. Giving more emphasis to your exhale is proven to calm your mind and body. Try extending your exhalation, it has a relaxing effect. Experiment with that.

When I go into meditation, I sometimes have visions, and it can be scary. What's going on with that?

Keeping your attention gently on your breath, may protect you from invasive thoughts. Do not allow yourself to be distracted by the relentless activity of your mind. When your mind is relaxed, it allows thoughts to arise, very much like dreams when you are sleeping. Try not to engage in, follow, or be attached to any ideas or images that arise. The time you set aside for meditation is your designated time to do nothing but focus on your breath. If an answer or solution to a problem arises—and it will—make a mental note of it and return your attention to the breath.

Sometimes a creative idea will come to us and get us excited and distract us from the practice. Again, thank the universe for its inspiration, make a mental note of the creative idea, and return your attention to your breath.

Any time you experience fear, you might affirm that you live in a safe and loving universe. See the next question below for information about dealing with fear and invoking the White Light of Protection. And finally, it cannot be overemphasized how helpful and important it is to have a teacher. Definitely reach out, find a qualified teacher to guide you and share whatever comes up that you are uncomfortable with during meditation.

And do not be afraid or stigmatized about talking to a counselor or mental health professional; seeking help is a sign of self-respect. Bringing scary things to light, out in the open, where they can be seen and talked about, reveals them for what they are, not monsters at all, but hidden aspects that are asking to be noticed.

Sometimes we can work through our difficulties on our own and sometimes we cannot. If your fears get worse, love yourself and give yourself a break. If meditation isn't working for you and makes you uncomfortable, do not continue.

I am a Christian and my doctor told me that meditation would be good for me. I want to be careful not to get wrapped up in Eastern religions or anything "New Age-y."

Here in the U.S.A., we need to be aware that meditation

for everyone does not include belonging to an Eastern religion or any religion. One definition of prayer is talking to God or telling God what you want. One definition for meditation is listening to God, who dwells within. By quieting ourselves so that we can listen, we may hear that still quiet voice that is God. As you are a Christian, enter the experience knowing that God or Jesus is with you and especially within you. When you breathe in you can silently say *God* or *Jesus* or *Spirit* or *Light*. I have heard some people say they breathe in goodness and exhale evil. I personally do not agree with that dualistic thinking, I feel that it amplifies fear and separation, which is all too prominent in this crazy world. Dwelling on duality and polarity is just the opposite of our goal!

Thinking in terms of good and evil, right or wrong, can get confusing since it is based on fear and judgment instead of love. Fear-based thinking can lead to hatred, violence, judgment, and war in our world. Christ taught universal, unconditional love for all things and forgiveness. Next time you feel yourself automatically judging something or someone, try forgiving them instead.

One of the side effects of meditation, if not a goal, is that the boundaries of separation dissolve. What happens with meditation is that clinging to our separate sense of self (or ego) dissolves. Having what the 12-Step programs call a *Higher Power* enables us to give up our lives to the will of something greater than we are. In the East this devotional practice is called *guru yoga*. With Jesus as the object of your devotion, you cannot go wrong.

It is interesting that neuroscience is studying the effects of religion, prayer, and meditation on our brains. Parts of our brains light up while we are in these states of oneness. The same effects occur whether we are in Buddhist or Hindu meditation, praying to Jesus, chanting the rosary with Mary or feeling the compassion of Kuan Yin.

Meditation may help all of us see the unity of all life and the interdependence of all phenomena. We can approach anything new in life with either curiosity or fear. For most of us our minds are uncharted territory; going within or even just being alone can be scary. Having a teacher or a guide is a great blessing to make you feel less fearful and alone. Think of Jesus as being with you to guide you in the process. Or you can invoke the angels, who are more than happy to help you; in fact, that is what they are here for and are delighted to be called upon. Your pastor or minister can guide you, too. If you still feel afraid or vulnerable when you meditate, it may be helpful to breathe in a protective White Light and surround yourself with it. This can purify and inspire you. It is called *enlightenment* for a reason!

Acknowledgments

Thank you to my parents, Mac and Vivian McCall and to all my teachers, starting in the first grade, for instilling in me a love of words and a love of learning. From Brian, my original TM teacher, my Taoist teacher, my yoga teachers, and all the Christian and Buddhist teachers I have studied with, my thanks are immeasurable.

Thank you to all the friends, students and professionals who have inspired me and have believed in me. Your support has meant so much. Thank you to Father Don Hyatt, who co-facilitated our little meditation group in his beautiful historic adobe church and asked me to type out instructions for beginners. In the beginning was the Word!

To those who have read this book and given me valuable suggestions and feedback— priceless! Robin Schumann told me and his friends that mine was the best book he had ever read about meditation. Robin and his mother, Marilee, then created a beautiful hand bound edition, complete with Marilee's original art for the cover. It is one of my most treasured possessions! Most of all, to hold a book in my hands that I had written gave me a felt sense of what it meant to be an author. Thank you so much.

Some who have read this manuscript have gone over and beyond anything I could have imagined, generously putting in countless hours, not just reading the book, but sharing pages and pages of notes, suggestions, insightful comments and professional experience. Most of all, Bo Bergström, Ellen Wood, Monique Parker, Genevieve Chavez Mitchell, Diana Tittle and Bonnie Currie: you have all helped make this book so much better! I especially thank the late, great John Nichols, author extraordinaire, whose ten pages of typewritten notes and cartoons about this book is a rollicking good read in itself.

Thank you to my sister and college roommate, Carol McCall, former English major, for all her big sisterliness — for tiptoeing respectfully as I meditate, lo, these many decades ago and supporting my meditation practice and everything that goes with it. The same is true for my super-hero, Pete Crider. Sharing a home with a heart of gold has been illuminating. He is a champion in every sense of the word, not just for me, but for everyone who knows him. He planted the seeds for this effort and watered and nurtured them all along the way.

Tremendous thanks go to the fearless Sara Martinez, my friend, agent and publisher for taking this work and actually turning it into a book! And for flinging it out into the wild blue yonder for the world to read.

And finally, thank you, dear reader, this is for you. As the Buddhists say, "May all beings benefit."

About the Author

Lou McCall grew up in New Mexico and became interested in nature, yoga and meditation at a young age. As a child she stumbled upon the book, "Yoga, Youth and Reincarnation" by Jess Stearn, which explained how to literally make clouds go away. So began Lou's interest in the mind and what it can do, an interest that continues to this day.

Lou has had a lifelong interest in comparative religions, spiritual psychology, and natural healing. A communitarian, she has devoted much of her life to organizing community projects and has worked closely with many non-profit organizations. An artist, activist, teacher, journalist and poet, this is her first book. Lou makes her home in rural New Mexico, where she and her partner and their animals enjoy a simple, creative lifestyle, with organic gardening, and eating good food being some of their favorite pastimes. Lou is a teacher of yoga and meditation. Her website is www.loumccall.com.

Praise for Meditation for Everyone

"Lou, I really enjoyed your book. It's lovely, simple and really gentle. I have never "meditated," per se, but you make it accessible, and non-complicated, non-convoluted, non- "technical," non-threatening. It really is for Everyone, and I like the fact that you call it a "secular guide"... and it triggered so much positive stuff, thoughts and memories for me."

—John Nichols, author

"The book is excellent. Truly. It's a great little primer that reminds me of the works of Thich Nhat Hahn as it shares the strengths of his writing: life wisdom imparted with calmness and clarity."

—Diana Tittle, Author

"What comes across so strikingly is Lou McCall's dedication to meditation, her strong belief in the power of contemplative practice and the capacity of each person to access his or her potential, no matter what their personality traits or circumstances might be."

—Russell G. Brown, M.D., psychiatrist

"...there's a gem on every page. Lou's approach is gentle and intriguing... I enjoyed every moment and learned so much. I feel much more confident of my meditations that began way back with no instructions, just the desire to sit in stillness. Her contribution is going to be enjoyed and appreciated by many."

—Linn Bayne, poet

"An easily digestible, concise entree into the practices and benefits of meditation that will impart morsels of wisdom to even the seasoned practitioner."

—Monique Parker, Yoga Therapist, Vedic Chanting Teacher

"I have to say, this was great reading! If I was someone looking to start meditation, or was a beginning student of meditation, this book would be invaluable. The prose flows effortlessly, and I was able to read the entire text in no time... This book accomplished what Lou McCall has set out to do!"

—Daoist teacher Xuan Wei

"This book is a menu for meditation, something for everyone."

—The Venerable Lama Karma Rinchen

MEDITATION CHECKLIST

Here are the seven points of meditation. Feel free to use this checklist to remind yourself until they become second nature!

☐ **Sitting**

☐ **Posture**

☐ **Shoulders and Arms**

☐ **Hands**

☐ **Neck and Chin**

☐ **Eyes**

☐ **Mouth**

www.ingramcontent.com/pod-product-compliance
Lightning Source LLC
LaVergne TN
LVHW051136080426
835510LV00018B/2440